How to Negotiate
Your First Job

How to Negotiate
Your First Job

8 Steps that will create value
for you and your new employer

To Wally —
With appreciation &
best wishes

Farzana Mohamed
Telluride June 2015

Paul F. Levy & Farzana S. Mohamed

Cover Design by Zahra Kanji
Layout Design by Moicher Sforim

ISBN: 978-0-9912714-1-2
ISBN: (Digital): 978-0-9912-7142-9

Printed in the United States of America

Process Improvement, LLC
negotiateyourjob.com

For our families, and the young people who inspire us.

CONTENTS

INTRODUCTION

Karim, soon to be a college graduate, was stunned into inaction, paralyzed by an unforeseen opportunity. In the midst of a recession, with an unemployment rate topping 9 percent, he had been offered a job.

The e-commerce company at which he had just spent the summer as a software design intern wanted to hire him. The rub? He thought he should be paid ten percent more than the offer.

With a semester of college left, he had several months to decide whether to accept the position, but he didn't know what to do next. Would they be insulted if he asked for more money? Would it sour his relationship with the person who made the offer? Was he allowed to talk with another company in which he was interested? Should he tell this company that he had another offer?

Karim is not alone in being inexperienced in the ways of the world when it comes to negotiating the terms of his first job. Many graduating college students have no idea what to do or say as they approach an employer. In fact, neither do many people who are already in the workforce.

This book is for the Karims of the world. You have spent most of your childhood and young adult life going to school–primary school, secondary school, and college–preparing to enter the work force. You have gotten pretty good at science, mathematics, computer programming, accounting, or whatever. You have applied for jobs or, like Karim, you have been offered a job out of the blue. Now, it is time to sit down face to face with your potential employer, and you don't know what to say and you don't know what to ask.

We are going to give you the tools to get through this stage of your life. Sure, we are going to help you get what you want and deserve. But, here's the little secret. We're going to help you get what you want and deserve in a way that will make your new employer even more pleased to hire you. "What?" you say, "I will end up with more money and better working conditions and my new employer will be happy?" That's right.

The principles on which this book is based are tried and true methods of expert negotiators. Even though you are not an expert negotiator, you can use them.

You have to be strategic in your approach and realize that the real negotiation begins well before you sit down face to face with your potential new employer. You also have to be mindful, aware of the process of the negotiation as it proceeds. As Bill Ury, one of the world's experts in negotiation likes to say: You must learn to stand on a balcony watching the negotiation and evaluating its progress, even as you participate in it.

And, believe it or not, we'll even show you how to take pleasure in the negotiation. While we cannot promise that it will be stress free, we can promise that you will learn from the experience and find joy in it. We can also promise that you will be a better and more valuable employee for your new firm as a result of the experience.

The approach set forth in this book is based on a few fundamental concepts of negotiation that we will explore in depth. As you gain an understanding of them, you will be able to use them to your advantage.

As an outline of what to expect in this book, we will introduce these negotiation concepts now, in shortened version. Later, we will explain them more fully and give examples, and we will teach you how to employ them.

Negotiation *is a* **means** *of advancing the full set of your* **interests** *by* **jointly decided action***. This is fundamental. If negotiating is a* **means** *to an end, we must consider alternatives to it. Talking about* **interests** *means that you have to give thought to and understand your interests. By* **jointly decided action***, we mean that both sides must agree. Therefore a negotiation is an exercise in solving a simultaneous equation.*

BATNA*—The "best alternative to a negotiated agreement." Simply stated, this is your other option. It serves as a benchmark during the negotiations to help you evaluate the offers and counteroffers made by a potential employer. That person also has a BATNA. This is the threshold value that any acceptable agreement must exceed. How do you evaluate your BATNA? How do you estimate theirs? What can you do to enhance your BATNA? What can you do to degrade theirs?*

Interest-based negotiation*—Positions and interests are two distinctly different concepts in a negotiation. How do you learn to distinguish between the two? How do you tease* *out their underlying interests, as opposed to the positions they put forth? How do you avoid locking yourself into a position that does not reflect your true interests?*

Trading on differences—*There are attributes of a negotiated agreement that have different values for the two parties. The difference in valuation offers the potential for an agreement that can add value for both parties. A good negotiation is not only about splitting the pie—it's about expanding the pie, with benefits to both parties. In negotiation parlance, this is called creating value.*

Tactics—*In addition to thinking strategically about the negotiation before you get to the table, there are tactical approaches that can help the conversation move along more productively when you are at the table.*

On the issue of gender—*It has been documented that women tend to do worse in negotiations, and especially negotiations about new jobs. We don't think this has to be the case, and we will explore this phenomenon. We'll talk about you, your gender, and your personality and figure out how to merge those characteristics into an effective approach to negotiation.*

For men and women, practice makes perfect—*We'll suggest how to apply the negotiating principles in this book to your daily life so that you're ready for the big deal. And, we'll provide tutorials on how to develop your own negotiating style.*

Before turning to these topics, we want to emphasize one very important point. We will never, in this book, ask you to engage in a practice that is unethical, immoral, disrespectful or irresponsible. We care about your reputation and your future, and you should too. The past casts a long shadow, and you should never do anything in a negotiation that does not meet "the mother test"—Would I be ashamed or feel awkward in describing to my mother what I have done or said?

That being the case, we will also ask you to be selfish in your negotiation. This is a not a time for altruism or for personal self-sacrifice. We want you to be pleased with the result of your negotiation. If you complete a deal but feel resentful, you will not have succeeded. By the way, your new employer wants the same for you. The last thing they need is a grouchy and angry new staff member. They want you to succeed and be a productive member of their team. We want you to do so, too, but we want you to have the best possible deal.

Finally, while the principles and strategies you'll learn in this book are specific to negotiating your first job offer, the lessons and concepts are also broadly applicable to the kinds of conversations and negotiations you'll encounter in your everyday life, as well as through the rest of your professional career.

We want your negotiation to be successful—for both you and your employer. We know, from our own experience and that of hundreds of others, that this is possible. We have strategies, approaches, and tools that can help make this so. This book will help get you there through a series of steps. As indicated above, these steps are based on sound negotiation theory, using principles that have been proven in all kinds of situations around the world. Some of these steps will be new to you and will require practice. Others will be intuitive, things you do naturally now. Indeed, you may be pleasantly surprised to learn that things you are already good at can be successfully employed in this new situation.

Who are we to offer this kind of advice? One of us is a seasoned administrator, the former CEO of several organizations, who has been involved in hiring dozens of professionals and who also has had to negotiate his own employment agreements. He is an internationally recognized expert in negotiation, conducting training of senior executives for many kinds of companies and institutions, and assisting corporate leaders in negotiation strategy for many kinds of business deals. The other is a younger professional, closer in age to many of you reading this book, who has had several managerial jobs and has successfully applied these methods during her tenure in the business world. In addition, she has provided helpful career planning and job negotiation advice to dozens of college seniors, graduate students, and young professionals in a variety of fields in the US, Canada, Europe and elsewhere. Both of us have collected anecdotes that we will share with you in the book, supplementing the powerful principles of negotiation with real-life examples.

Ok, let's get down to business and help you secure a great job!

STEP 1:

Decide to Negotiate

It might seem kind of silly to suggest to you—in a book about how to negotiate your first job—that the first step is to decide to negotiate.

But many people don't. Especially people like you who are just finishing college and are really happy to get a job. You may be worried that the employer will get angry or upset if you quibble over the terms of the job they've just offered you. Maybe you are worried that they will withdraw the offer, and you will be back to square one. You imagine the worst: You might even have to move back in with your parents after graduation!

It may help to take a look at this from the other side. Here's a summary from a friend about the process used by his company to hire an entry-level analyst:

- *We spent thousands of dollars to hire a professional search firm to screen dozens of resumes.*
- *Our team members conducted about 15 total phone screens of promising candidates. Each interview took 30 to 45 minutes.*

- *We brought in about 8 candidates for in-person interviews to meet several members of our team, each of whom spent 45 minutes to an hour with each candidate.*
- *We chose two candidates to give a case presentation to the entire partnership.*
That's 12 partners who spent over an hour listening to each of two presentations.
- *Then we made an offer to our first choice, and after a few discussions around expectations, the initial offer was accepted.*

What's wrong with this picture? The last phrase: "The initial offer was accepted."

The candidate didn't even try to explore whether there could have been a better agreement.

Once an employer has offered you a job, they clearly want you. They've likely spent thousands of dollars and hundreds of hours choosing you.

The second-place candidate may not have made the grade. If you don't take the job, the employer might have to start over again.

Moreover, they really want you to work for them and not their competitors. They thought you were the best in class. The last thing they want is for you to work for the competition.

This means you have leverage, something many first-time job seekers don't realize. You can use this leverage to negotiate a better deal than their initial offer. Many prospective employers actually anticipate that you will to try to make a deal.

Mary Markel Murphy, who does recruitment for MIT, said, "You need to know that it is okay and even expected that you negotiate. As an HR professional, I leave a little buffer room when I make an offer with the expectation that a candidate may negotiate and I may need to increase the salary offer as a result."

Kate, a very accomplished professional who has hired lots of people during her career, said:

"Recognize that the offer is the entry, not the final offer. *Always* ask for more. Be creative: More vacation, more service accrual, more money, more bonus, something deferred, some training or education perk. Don't be embarrassed to ask for more. Act like you are negotiating for someone else. This is not personal. It is business."

Regrets if You Don't Negotiate

What happens if you don't try to negotiate a better deal? The good news is that you will have a job. The bad news is that you may find out later that your colleagues did better than you. This could make you feel angry or resentful—maybe even a bit stupid—and you don't want to feel that way when you have an otherwise exciting and interesting job.

You also will come to realize that you have short-changed yourself in other aspects of your life.

Sally's experience is all too common: "Being a new grad, I had no idea of how much value I was bringing the company. I saw it as them doing me a favor by giving me a job. I valued interesting work way more highly than getting paid well, so I didn't pay much attention to this. I was just excited about working on neat stuff."

It was only later that she understood the implications of her decision not to negotiate:

"I didn't realize how much your first salary affects the rest of your life, i.e., future raises, when you can buy your first house, your 401k savings (since they're a percentage of salary), and your credit rating."

She said with regret:

"I didn't understand that a few thousand dollars was insignificant to these companies relative to the value of a good employee or even a decent employee."

Kaitlin, an extremely successful person in the bio-tech field, had a similar theme: "Failing to negotiate puts you behind others in pay and title, and it is really hard to catch up over time, even when companies like mine make an effort to do so with annual pay increases."

You shouldn't have to start out your career with this sort of regret, especially once you understand that you are in a position to do better for yourself. (This doesn't mean, though, that you should be greedy or misuse your leverage. If you do, you might end up living with your parents!)

We've noticed, however, that even people who are convinced of their worth may have a deep prejudice against negotiation. They equate it with haggling. In negotiation-speak, they view it solely as claiming value: "I am going to get as much as possible out of you. I will win and you will lose."

Perhaps you have been through that kind of haggling— a single transaction like buying a used car—that has left you feeling used and taken advantage of. You might have felt resentful about the result. Or worse, stupid. "Why on earth did I agree to pay that much for such a wreck of a car?"

These feelings are often the result of bad preparation, failure to create the proper aspirations for the negotiating process, or perhaps misunderstanding the context within which the talks are happening. Just like other problems you have faced in your life, these are elements that you can fix.

You can have a respectful, thoughtful, and collegial discussion with your potential employer that will get you a better result. Such a conversation might produce a better financial package with a higher salary, signing bonus or performance bonuses. Or maybe it will result in better working conditions that help you advance—like training, travel or enhanced responsibilities. The discussion could also garner lifestyle improvements for you, such as vacation time, flexible working hours and the ability to work from home.

Here's the magic part: You can conduct a negotiation in a manner that not only enhances your situation but also brings additional value to the company, making your employer even happier that they have chosen you to join their firm.

But you have to decide to negotiate.

The next steps will show you how.

True-Life Story: Joyce Murphy

A friend and colleague of mine was contacted by an executive search firm and ultimately recruited to a very senior executive position in health care. When talking with her during the process, she explained to me that she was convinced they were about to make her an offer and she was ready to accept. I asked her if they had discussed salary, benefits, etc. and she said they had not gotten into the details yet but the search firm had given her a number that they believed she would be offered. She then quickly added, "And I am going to accept!"

I asked, "What do you mean, you will accept their first offer?" She replied that she has never in her career asked for more than the original offer. I was stunned. This is a woman who is a lawyer by training, has served in general counsel positions and has been an executive leader for a number of years. She has negotiated amazing deals for her company and for many with whom she has worked…and…she is proudly telling me she has never asked for more than what has been offered to her and she will do the same this time.

I almost fell off my chair. I said, "That is ridiculous. The first offer is just that, the first offer, a starting point from which to negotiate." I said, "No one accepts the first offer." Anyway, we then talked about the salary. I told her it is so easy to get salary info, and we need to get that information on this company as well as comps. I also asked about benefits, moving expenses, etc., and we spent a fair amount of time developing a proposed counter-offer. She ultimately negotiated a very good package that was competitive and appropriate given the market.

STEP 2:

Building a Trusting Relationship

If you go to Africa, India, or the Middle East—or to a shop run by someone from that part of the world—you may witness a powerful negotiation strategy.

The shop owner invites you in for a cup of tea.

"You don't have to buy anything," he assures you.

You enter the rug shop or the sari shop confident that you are not going to buy anything. You leave an hour or more later, bundles in hand, feeling that you got a real bargain.

What's happening here?

The proprietor of the store—who full well intends to sell you something at the highest possible price—does not start the process by haggling over some item. He gently seduces you into a comfortable chair, offers you some delicious mint tea or jasmine tea and biscuits, and starts talking about you and your family. Before you know it, you have revealed all kinds of information to him. And he to you. Eventually, you say something that indicates an interest in a particular product. At that point, he brings out the rolls of cloth and starts to show you many, many samples. He patiently brings out more and more samples, learning about your preferences—color, texture, design— refining what he shows you until you see something you can't live without.

Only then does the price discussion take place. He anchors your expectations by letting you see the price tag on the item, but he almost immediately draws a contrast with that price by announcing that he is pleased to be able to offer you a substantial discount. Even though you start haggling over the price, the discussion is collegial—even good-humored. After all, you have just shared tea and biscuits and your family history with him. You are practi- cally friends!

The conclusion is virtually inevitable. If this seller has done his job well, you buy, but you feel good about what you bought. You might even say to friends later, "You should go to Ahmed's shop. He's got a great selection and he's really fair."

Ahmed has a lesson for all of us. Negotiations go better when the two parties have a relationship. Why? Later in this book, we offer some advice especially to women about negotiating. But the basic premise of that section of the book—that there is both ease and value to be gained in personalizing the negotiation by creating a relationship—applies to both men and women.

The reason you don't want to jump right in and start haggling about the terms of an offer right after getting it is because this can set off a "flight or fight" response. It puts the other person on the defensive and sets you up to be an adversary rather than a partner in reaching an agreement.

You may appear too hard-nosed or overly aggressive. Such an approach also limits your ability to learn more about your employer's interests, a key step to creating more value for both of you.

In contrast, a discussion on terms that follows a more general discourse about other topics—topics that permit the two of you to get to know one another better—can feel more collegial and collaborative.

The good news for you is you have probably already established some relationships as part of your hiring process. You have been through one or two or more interviews. The folks hiring you like you well enough to want you as part of their firm. So you have a leg up on the negotiation process.

However, negotiating the terms of your employment is different from interviewing, so you should expect that you will need to develop the relationship further. The items about which you are talking are very different in nature from the ones you discussed when they were considering you for the job. It is not unusual for a manager to feel uncomfortable about discussing the terms of the job. It is also not unusual for that person to feel initial constraints about what he or she can offer you.

In some cases, you may be negotiating with a human resources administrator or another person whom you did not meet during the interview process. You will need to establish some kind of rapport with this person, just as you did with those who interviewed you earlier.

So try this. Once an offer has been made—and before you respond to it—find something personal to talk about.

If it is someone you have already met, the conversation might go like this:

"Before we get to that, do you mind if I ask you a few questions? As you know, I am new to the job market, and it would help me get a better perspective."

The reply is likely to be, "Sure. What did you have in mind?"

You might then ask such questions that you didn't address in the interview such as, "When you were my age, what were you hoping for in your first job?" "How did it work out?" "What did you learn that might be helpful to me?"

After some back and forth, you can bring the discussion back to the offer: "As you know, I am really excited about working with you. If you don't mind, I have some questions about the offer you have presented." Then proceed.

There may come a point when the person on the other side of the table feels discomfort, wanting to give you what you have asked for, but finding it outside of his allowed range. At that point, you could say, "I understand this is a bit unusual. Are there any ideas I can provide that might help you explain it within the company so we can get approval?"

We? Yes, you have now gone from sitting across the table (figuratively) from your possible boss to sitting on the same side. You are colleagues trying to figure out the best way to get what you both want from others in the firm. Such collaboration would be extremely unlikely without a sense of a personal relationship, a sense that you have helped to create by your approach to the negotiation.

The situation is slightly different if the person who is making the offer is someone with whom you have not interviewed because you don't have a relationship, and you have to start from scratch.

Again, instead of diving in to discuss terms, start off by asking questions that will help you get to know this person and maybe learn a little more about the company:

"How long have you worked here?" "Why did you join?" "What do you like about the place?" "Where are you from?"

As she answers, look for areas of common interest. Respond to her comments and engage in a conversation. She's likely to ask you questions about yourself too. You should find yourself smiling a lot, and she will be too.

Eventually, you will say, "I'm really excited about the opportunities here and would love to be a part of the place. I have a few questions about the offer, though, and am hoping you can explain some things to me."

At this point, she will be open to helping you. Her job, after all, is to close the deal.

You could say something like, "I've looked at the salary offer and I've compared it to what I am seeing in the industry, and it looks a bit lower. I'm sure your firm wants to be competitive in this kind of market. Can you please explain the thought behind this offer?"

[Her thoughts: "Wow, I can see why they want this person to work here!"]

She is now much more likely to warmly work with you and come to terms that are better for you and the company.

In the following chapters, we will provide specific negotiation strategies and techniques, but remember that all of them will work a lot better if you have taken the time to establish a trusting relationship with your counterpart.

Having that relationship will make you more comfortable in advocating for yourself. The relationship will also make it more likely that the other party will share important information with you and will feel a desire to advocate on your behalf.

You will find it easier to build that relationship if you are confident in your position, you know what you are worth, and what is reasonable to expect. It is to those items that we now turn.

STEP 3:

Know Your BATNA, and Theirs

Let's start by reminding ourselves of a key point: If you are at the point of negotiating the terms of a new job, the employer has decided that they want you. Yes, you. They may have gone through an extensive hiring process and interviewed dozens of people. There is something about your experience, your knowledge, your skills, and your personality that has made them decide that you are the right person for the job. They want you to join their team, and they certainly don't want you going to the competition.

If we think about the job negotiation in that light, we can imagine that you are on the same side as your future employer. They want to hire you. You want to be hired. The negotiation is a way of framing things so that you are working together to come up with a package that's good for both sides. As we have said above, our goal in this book is to help you have a conversation that gets you more of what you want, but does it in such a way that the employer is even happier about hiring you than before the negotiation took place.

It might seem odd, therefore, that an important step as you plan for the negotiation is to think about your alternative to accepting the job. As discussed earlier, in negotiation parlance, we call this "the no-deal alternative." The shorthand term we use for it is *BATNA*, your **Best Alternative To a Negotiated Agreement**.

Remember, negotiation is a means to an end. In this case, the "end" is your happiness. If you are conducting a negotiation and conclude that you will feel better by not making the deal, you should walk away. We'll want to remember, too, that while happiness may relate to money, it also is likely to comprise other factors.

For now, though, let's look at a simple financial analogy. Imagine that you are going to an auction, excited to bid on an item of interest. The auctioneer starts the bidding, and you jump in, raising the offer as you compete against others in the room. At the end, you win, but then you realize that you have agreed to a bid that exceeds the amount of money you have in your bank account.

Of course, this is crazy. You would never think of participating in an auction without knowing your financial limit. But people often do the equivalent when they enter into a job negotiation. They find themselves in a conversation for which they have not fully prepared.

The auction scenario is a kind of negotiation. If your bid is the highest, you win, and you agree to purchase at that price. There is an alternative to "winning" in this case. We call it "losing," but if the winning bid is going to exceed your net worth, you haven't really "lost." You have made a choice. You have decided that walking away is more pragmatic than reaching an agreement.

Before beginning a negotiation, you want to understand your BATNA—the scenario or course of action that you would pursue if there is no deal with the other person. Your job is to "price" your BATNA to see if it makes more sense than the offer on the table. Why? If we view negotiation as a means to a goal, such as having financial stability, we must also consider other means available to you to reach that end. This could be a competing job offer, or it may be the expectation of another offer, or even the option of doing something else with your time such as starting a venture or continuing school.

You want to constantly evaluate the process and likely result of the negotiation against your other options. Knowing your BATNA will tell you the point at which you are just indifferent between saying "yes" and walking away.

For example, consider selling a used car. You need the cash, and the only important thing to you is how much you can get for the vehicle. You do a little research and learn that the Blue Book value for your car—what you can reasonably expect to be paid for it on the open market—is $4,500. A local car dealer has offered you a firm bid of $4,000. A prospective buyer responds to your ad on Craigslist. She offers you $3,800 and says, "I won't pay a penny more."

Because you have done your homework, you know that your best alternative—your BATNA—is at least $4,000, which is the dealer's offer. You may even be able to get more if you wait for more replies to your ad.

So although you might like to make a deal with your prospective buyer, if you believe her $3,800 offer is firm, you have to turn it down as being worse than your BATNA.[1]

_____

1   In this example, we have purposefully made money the only criterion that matters. If you say that there are other considerations that matter to

The BATNA is the threshold value that any acceptable agreement must exceed. But recall that a negotiated agreement is a jointly decided action. The other party also has a BATNA, a maximum price limit. If the maximum they are willing to pay you is greater than the minimum you are willing to accept, a deal is possible. We call that interval—the space between their maximum and your minimum—a *ZOPA*, a **Zone of Possible Agreement**.

Here's how it looks mathematically:

[Their Maximum > Your Minimum] = ZOPA

But if their maximum is less than your minimum, there is no ZOPA, and no agreement is possible. Here's what that looks like mathematically:

[Their Maximum < Your Minimum] ≠ ZOPA

As you negotiate your first job, your task is to think about how to evaluate your BATNA and how to estimate theirs. But here is a key point: If you wait until you are at the bargaining table to conduct your BATNA analysis, you will not achieve as good a result as if you engage in some research beforehand. While you will learn things at the table, we want you to behave strategically—to plan before you act. Great strategists prepare in advance. Indeed, it is likely that you will want to spend more time working on the negotiation away from the table than you will at the table.

---

you, then your BATNA might be a bit different. For example, if you are swayed by the prospective buyer's appearance and want a date—and you think a lower price might help your social life—well, that's something else. Maybe sacrificing a few hundred dollars on the purchase price is worth it! We'll get back to that point later when we talk about understanding the full set of your interests.

We know that your decision to take or not take a job is based on more than money. But for a moment, let's spend some time on a simplified salary negotiation to illustrate how to employ a strategic approach to the BATNA question.

How do you evaluate your BATNA? You want to make a salary that is in line with your level of education and experience, and you think it should be at least as good as other jobs in the marketplace. But how do you know what that dollar range is?

If this is your only job offer and you don't have a specific proposal from some other company against which to compare it, you will have to do a bit of research. Even if you have a couple of offers, this research will help you evaluate them. In the used car example, you could have turned to the Blue Book, looked at ads that you have seen online or elsewhere, or talked to friends who have recently bought or sold a car. In the employment world, there are similar points of reference.

Go to the Internet and see what you can learn about salary ranges for any particular job. Look for resources such as Salary.com and Glassdoor.com. Search for newspaper stories about labor markets, job conditions, and salary ranges. See if your college career services office has information about salary ranges and benefits.

Don't limit yourself to online resources, however. Talk with your friends and friends of friends, those graduating this year and those who entered the workforce last year. Many colleges have rich alumni networks; don't be afraid to reach out to someone in your industry to ask questions. But recognize that it can be awkward to ask a person what he or she makes. Likewise, if you say, "What do you think

I'm worth?" the person you call may feel uncomfortable about answering directly. So, an indirect way to phrase the question is, "What is the range of starting salaries a person could expect in this company (or field)?"

All of that research helps you understand your BATNA and helps you narrow down the range of the price associated with it.

The numbers you come up with might be different depending on where you live. They also might vary depending on the specific experience and expertise that you bring to the job. But at least you now have an idea of a reasonable range of possible salaries.

While you are evaluating your BATNA, understand that your prospective employer has probably done the same thing. After all, they are trying to recruit great prospects like you, and they know they have to offer salaries in the range of the market. But they might also face important constraints on how much they can offer. Both big and small firms often have salary schedules that they use when recruiting new folks. They do this so their overall salary distribution—between new staff and incumbents—doesn't get out of whack.

In the next chapter, we will deal with what you can do to enhance your BATNA and, interestingly, what you can do to degrade their BATNA. In so doing, you might be able to create a ZOPA where there appeared to be none, or you might be able to influence the other party's assessment of the ZOPA to your advantage. For instance, if the other party thinks that you have a credible competing offer, their understanding of their BATNA will start to shift in your favor, opening up a broader range of possible agreement.

For now, let's think about the actions you want to take

before and during your negotiation:

1. *Before sitting at the table,* learn as much as you can about your BATNA and their BATNA. Get a feeling for the true ZOPA (zone of possible agreement). Use publicly available sources of data and information. Talk to friends and colleagues.

2. *While sitting at the table,* supplement what you have learned about your BATNA and their BATNA by listening carefully and asking questions.

3. *Always remember that they really want you to join the company.* You are negotiating with them, not against them. Try to maintain a conversational approach and help frame the entire discussion as a joint problem-solving activity, not an adversarial proceeding.

Is it hard to walk away from an offer when you don't have another one? You bet! But it can sometimes be the right path to take. Look at this next real-life story. Laura-Lynne helps us understand that you shouldn't "settle" unless or until you just have to. She also reminds us that doing pre-negotiation research about the market is important in helping you evaluate an offer.

True-Life Story: Laura-Lynne

After moving to California and looking for work for months, Laura-Lynne found a temporary position, working at a decent sized newspaper. Within a short time, she was offered a full-time job. It was a rare opportunity given the dearth of jobs and the abundance of candidates.

Laura-Lynne felt lucky to have the offer, but it was on the low end of the scale. Although she was worried about blowing the offer, Laura-Lynne was more concerned about her long-term financial future. She approached the issue with a carefully worded response. Rather than asking for a specific number, she said she appreciated the offer but was concerned about the salary given the cost of living in the area and given that her future pay at the paper would be tied to that starting salary and was there room to do any better.

The editor who was doing the hiring said she understood and would talk to her boss. The next day she came back with an offer that was even more than Laura-Lynne had hoped for. The editor apologized that it wasn't more and offered her an extra week of vacation. As a side note, Laura-Lynne said if they'd come back and said it was the best they could do, she would have taken the job anyway.

Laura-Lynne said the experience showed her that it was just business and not personal. The original offer wasn't really tied to how much the editor who was hiring her thought she was worth. They were just trying to get by as cheaply as possible.

STEP 4:

Influence Their Perception of the ZOPA

If you go into a salary negotiation and insist on getting paid $70,000 but the most the company can pay for your level of qualifications is $55,000, there is a chance that there is no ZOPA. Your minimum acceptable offer appears to exceed their maximum ability to pay.

But even here, maybe not.

Here's where influencing their perception of the ZOPA by degrading their BATNA and enhancing your BATNA comes into play. An illustration:

Employer: Jo, we are so happy at the prospect of having you join us that we are prepared to offer you $55,000.

Jo: Thank you so much. I am very excited about this firm, the people here, and the mission, and I appreciate your confidence that I could contribute to the success of a great organization. However, I am a bit surprised by your salary offer because it seems low compared to the rest of the industry. I imagine than it is important to you to be in the same range as your competitors.

Employer: Well, yes, we want to be in the market. We have consultants who tell us what the comparables are like. But, what kind of numbers are you seeing?

Jo: I have seen reliable documentation of salaries in the range of $70,000 for this kind of job in comparable firms. If you like, I can bring in some of that documentation.

Employer: Wow, that's hard for us. We have a salary schedule that would put that at the upper end for this job category. We have to be concerned about how our incumbents would feel if someone new came in at that level.

Jo: I understand completely, and I wouldn't ever want you to do anything that would cause morale problems internally. After all, I also want to have good relationships with my fellow workers and would hate for them to be resentful of me. Does your salary schedule make allowances for special attributes and experience of new staff? What if we were to explore some of the extra things I would bring to the company that might be of importance?

Employer: Well, I guess we could talk about that. What kinds of things do you mean?

Jo: It may not have been clear from my resume, but a major project I did for a professor last year included development of software that is directly applicable to the needs of this company. I could bring that expertise to bear with virtually no learning curve. We might be able to accelerate the delivery of your new product offering by several months because of what I bring to the organization.

Employer: Wow, I hadn't realized that. Sure, that could make a big difference.

Without threatening or demanding, and while being respectful—Jo is able to influence the employer's perception of the ZOPA because she has done her research and thought strategically about how she will use what she has learned. The perceived ZOPA has changed in two ways: First, the company's perception of its BATNA has been degraded and, second, their perception of Jo's capabilities has been enhanced and therefore her BATNA has improved.

Degrading their BATNA

Let's review what has happened. First, Jo has degraded the employer's perception of their own BATNA by pointing out that the salary that has been offered is low relative to the market. Because she has done the research, she can offer to provide documentation of this.

Importantly, Jo has not threatened to walk away: You are better off avoiding threats. They are counterproductive, especially with regard to relationships. Nonetheless, the way that Jo presented the factual case of the matter—the differential in salaries—suggests that she could go elsewhere and earn more. Why does it matter that she might walk away? Well, recall that the employer has already gone through an extensive and expensive recruitment process: Advertising, interviewing, checking references. This takes time and money. Indeed, a major cost for most businesses is their cost of recruitment, and they are sensitive to this cash outflow.

Also, and maybe even more important, recall that Jo is at the salary stage of negotiations because the folks in the company have decided that they really want her to join them. Besides not wanting to start over with a new search process, they don't want to lose their top choice—especially to a competitor. If we think about it, this is not a negotiation of Jo *versus* the company. This is a negotiation of Jo *with* the company, where they both seek a mutually acceptable outcome. Oddly enough, the person with whom you are discussing salary is on your side. He wants you to join, and he wants to give you enough money to make a deal. In degrading the other party's BATNA, you paradoxically are helping them satisfy their interests. In a take-off of the old Burger King advertisement, you are discovering the art of "letting them have your way."

Another potential advantage for job prospects is that recruiters are often judged by how quickly they close the deal with the firm's top job prospects. A colleague of ours worked at a major consulting firm. Once interviews were over and the firm had decided on their top candidate, it was Mark's job to close the deal. If the candidate had not signed on within a couple of weeks, Mark would get impatient calls from his boss: "What's going wrong? Don't lose this person to our competitors!"

Now, Mark's *own* performance was being evaluated. It was in his interest to dial up the salary offer a bit or come up with some other benefit to entice the candidate to accept.

Enhancing your BATNA

In addition to degrading the company's perception of its BATNA, Jo has simultaneously enhanced their perception of her abilities, and thereby her own BATNA. At the start of the conversation, Jo was just a run-of-the-mill software engineer, worthy of a certain salary. By the end, she has helped the company person understand that she brings some extra value compared to the normal recruit, helping the company achieve a market advantage. The firm now has reason to believe that Jo could deliver similar expertise to another company and would be able to command a higher salary elsewhere. By expanding the ZOPA in this direction, Jo has given the company a reason to overcome the issue of the internal salary schedule, providing a principled and concrete reason to offer the job at a higher pay level.

Note, too, the conversational manner in which Jo asks questions and makes comments.

First, she maintains a very positive attitude about wanting to join the company. This friendly approach reinforces the recruiter's belief that he has found the right person.

Second, she is respectful of the concerns and problems that the company faces. This is good manners and indicates that she is empathic, something that pays dividends in many ways. Her manner and approach suggest to the company person that Jo is going to be a good team player, again reinforcing their belief that they have found the right person. (Also, by the way, if you do join the company, those will be your concerns and problems, too.)

Third, she avoids the use of "yes-no" questions. For some psychological reason, "yes-no" questions tend to prompt a "no," cutting off a line of discussion that might be fruitful. Instead, Jo asked, "What if we were to explore …" It is very hard for the other party to turn down an open-ended invitation like that, especially if they really want to make a deal with you. A "what if" question invites the other party to engage in joint problem solving. You figuratively move from being *across the table* from each other to sitting *side by side*.

Here's a true story from the 1970s. Bob and his two best buddies were graduating from the MBA program at Harvard Business School. They all received job offers from one of the country's best management consulting firms. They were offered $55,000 as a starting salary. In that era, each person's personal goal was to see how quickly they could "make their age," i.e., be paid an amount in thousands equal to their chronological age. So to get $55,000 in one's early twenties was a good deal! Plus, the firm told them that the salary was not negotiable. They started work, and all three were assigned to the San Francisco office, where they took an apartment together.

The three did well in their jobs, and a year later, they were talking about their forthcoming annual reviews and how much they could hope for as a salary boost. One of the young men, Steve, said, "Yeah, I wonder how much of an increase I can expect from $60,000?"

Bob and his buddy said, "$60,000! How'd you get that? We got $55,000, and we were told it was not negotiable."

Steve said, "Everything is negotiable. I just pointed out that I was a Baker Scholar [someone in the top 5% of the class at HBS] and asked how much extra I would get paid for that. They offered $5000 more, and I accepted."

Steve understood how to introduce information into the salary negotiation that enhanced the company's perception of his BATNA.

Money has different forms

Our story about Jo has been a highly simplified example, if for no other reason than we have only focused on salary. In reality, however, there will clearly be other aspects of the deal that will be important to both you and the company. We limited the dialogue above to emphasize the need to think strategically while also giving you some tactical hints about how to participate in the negotiation discussion.

Note, too, that we didn't necessarily resolve the salary issue. What if, in spite of everything, the most the company could pay as a starting salary was $68,000? Should Jo walk away because her BATNA was $70,000? Maybe not. First of all, we are not sure that her BATNA really is $70,000 because Jo doesn't have a firm offer from another company. Second, Jo's other interests—vacation time, professional advancement opportunities—might be more important than the starting salary. Third, on the money front, there might be other options. Let's jump back into the discussion to illustrate this latter point.

Employer: This has been a great meeting, and I am confident I can get you a starting salary of $68,000, but I can't do better because of internal salary equity issues.

Jo: Thank you so much. I now understand your limitations on the starting salary. I am still a bit concerned about market comparables for this level of work. But perhaps we could explore some other options. What's your policy with regard to signing bonuses?

Here, Jo is again empathic and respectful but is also exploring a possible way of inventing more money that is consistent with the company's policies. Note that she doesn't say, "Will you pay me a signing bonus?" The question is not framed as "yes or no." It is framed respectfully as, "What is your policy?" Let's look at the two possible responses:

Case 1

Employer: Well, we usually don't offer those.

Jo: Oh, I am surprised, because I have often seen those used in the industry.

Employer: Well, let me check with our HR folks and see what might be possible.

Jo: That would be terrific. Thank you. When should we talk again?

Here is another important lesson. The deal does not have to be consummated in one meeting. Jo has raised a new issue—signing bonuses—that relates to how well this company competes in the marketplace for new staff people. She has employed another piece of research in an attempt to degrade the company's BATNA, but she is patient and comfortable about letting the company spend some time digesting and responding to the new information. It is often the case that a party who has been told that their BATNA is worse than expected will need some time to internalize that fact and come back to the table.

Case 2 (or the follow-up meeting from Case 1)

Employer: We sometimes offer signing bonuses under certain circumstances.

Jo: What if we were to explore whether the right circumstances might apply in this case?

Employer: Let me talk with our folks and see what might be possible. They might be nervous, though, that you would take the money and then choose to leave.

Jo: That's certainly not my plan! But if it would help, please let them know that I understand that the signing bonus might not be actually paid until I have been in the job for several months and you are content with my performance.

Employer: Good idea!

Again, Jo and the employer are now involved in jointly scheming to see how Jo could qualify for the signing bonus. As in Case 1, this might not get resolved right away. The employer might have to check with other people in the firm, but he will do so as an advocate for Jo, not as someone looking to say "no."

To summarize, ZOPAs are changeable. If you do your research well, you can employ facts to help the employer understand why their offer is not as good as something you could get elsewhere. You can help them understand that your BATNA is better than they might have originally thought, or that their BATNA is worse than they thought. But the manner in which you conduct this kind of conversation is extremely important. Respect, thoughtfulness, careful listening, patience, and good humor are essential ingredients in maintaining the kind of relationship that will help you get what you deserve. Arrogance, pettiness, sarcasm, threats, and anger will lead to a very short discussion—even to the point of having an offer withdrawn.

Let's summarize your tasks with regard to the ZOPA:

While sitting at the table, take actions to influence their perceptions of the ZOPA by degrading their perception of their BATNA and enhancing their perception of your own. In so doing:

- Avoid threats;
- Provide credible information and facts;
- Be respectful and empathic;
- Avoid "yes-no" questions;
- Be patient and give the other party time to incorporate their changed BATNA into their offer.

Real-life story: Gretchen Becker

In my personal case, I chose the job where I felt the work, the culture, and the hiring manager were the best fit for me, but one that also offered a salary that exceeded the minimum salary requirement I had set for myself given my goal of living on my own and supporting myself. I now realize that I sold myself a little short thinking that my lack of "real business experience" gave me little basis for negotiation.

Later, I felt like I had missed an opportunity to demonstrate how some of my unpaid experiences prepared me for the new job. I didn't connect my volunteer work as a college campus tour guide as relevant to the sales position for which I was applying. I "sold" my college to prospective freshmen and didn't even realize that I had sales experience! I was also a varsity soccer player in college but never discussed that in the interview process. Every employer is looking for an employee who is not only competitive but also a team player who can push herself through challenging or difficult situations and is willing to put in the time and effort to improve. I have drawn those analogies between my athletic accomplishments and the job requirements many times in subsequent interviews and salary negotiations, and I look for and value those qualities in the employees I'm hiring.

Know what you bring to the table in your knowledge, experience, and connections, and don't be afraid to sell them. The prospective employee who can articulate how his or her knowledge or experience will make them a high performer in the role, or support the company's goals and mission, is the employee who has more strength in the negotiation. Now is not the time to be modest, but you must tie your strengths and experience to the job requirements. To do this, you must do some research to understand the company's direction and the known requirements of the job. Don't be afraid to ask in the interview process what attributes have made people successful in the role in the past, and then find opportunities to share stories that demonstrate that you possess those same attributes. You don't want to just be a good fit for the job, you want to assure your prospective employer that you will be a high performer in that job.

One other point that should be noted is that sometimes the relevant experience you bring to the job and the negotiation isn't always obvious from your resume. I've hired athletes, not-for-profit fundraisers, and a former stay-at-home mom who was re-entering the workforce, all with little experience in my industry. In those cases I was convinced by them that their roles as a team player and competitor, or manager of a family and a home, prepared them for the requirements of the job for which I was hiring. Be prepared with stories of your experiences and how they prepared you for success in the role for which you are negotiating.

STEP 5:

Know Your Interests, and Theirs

In their seminal book on negotiation, *Getting to Yes*, Roger Fischer and Bill Ury tell this story:

> *After the 1967 Six-Day War in the Middle East, President Jimmy Carter invited the adversaries to Camp David to try to help the Egyptians and Israelis achieve a peace treaty. A major issue in contention was the Sinai Peninsula, which Israel had captured during the war. Egypt's position was, "We want it back. It belongs to Egypt." Israel's position was, "No way. If we give it back, you will use it as a staging area to amass troops, and you will attack us again."*
>
> *Carter understood that there were underlying interests of more importance than these positions. Egypt's interest was sovereignty based on a pride of ownership going back centuries. Israel's interest was national security. The solution emerged: Let the Egyptian flag fly over the Sinai to enable national pride to reemerge, but declare the peninsula to be a*

demilitarized zone so that Israel would not have to worry about another surprise attack.

This is a perfect illustration of the difference between positional bargaining and interest-based negotiation. Positional bargaining occurs when we get stuck with the description of something we say we need. In interest-based negotiation, we focus on what we really care about. Very often, it is something quite different from what we say we need.

Why does this matter to you in your job negotiation? If we think strategically about your objectives, there are probably a lot of things that matter to you just as much as salary. How you choose to put those forth and use them in the negotiation is very important to your ultimate satisfaction with the job. Both you and your employer want you to be satisfied, and so you want to share your interests with the employer as you discuss whether or not you will take the job.

But the employer also has important underlying interests, and it will help you to know what they are. Remember these important phrases from the Introduction:

*Negotiation is a means of advancing the **full set of your interests** by jointly decided action. By jointly decided action, we mean that both sides must agree. Therefore a negotiation is an exercise in solving a simultaneous equation.*

As we did in the last chapter with regard to our salary BATNA, it is helpful to think about your interests before you get to the bargaining table. It's not that you cannot and should not refine your understanding during the negotiation, but the bargaining table is not always the best place to do so. Sitting face to face across a table is stressful, and you are likely to be thinking about other things. So let's do the bulk of the work away from the table. Just as you plan and prepare ahead for the interviewing phase of your job search, rehearsing possible responses, you'll find that by preparing for and practicing how to talk with an employer, your job offer will pay dividends.

Start by thinking about the things that matter to you that have nothing to do with your soon-to-be current salary. What personal concerns have to be solved that would make you satisfied about a job if money were not an issue? You can even go to the extreme: Do your own "mind experiment" and pretend you are not going to be paid at all. What interests would have to be addressed to make you sure you wanted the job? Hey, that's really not so strange. After all, didn't you just go through several years of college education, where you paid money rather than getting paid? You probably wanted your chosen college to satisfy your interests, and you chose your school in great measure on that basis. You may even have taken unpaid internships during your college years to gain experience and opportunities to hone new skills or explore new fields.

Take some time to write down your interests

Here are some possibilities:

I am interested in ...

- The opportunity to learn new things.
- Moving up in the organization and taking on more and more responsibility.
- Getting an advanced degree.
- Living in a lot of different cities.

- Traveling.
- Living only in one city.
- Not traveling very much.
- Building my personal wealth.
- Having a flexible daily and weekly work schedule.
- Working at nighttime.
- Taking vacations whenever I want.

You may have others. The key to a successful negotiation, though, is to figure out how to merge your interests as much as possible with those of your employer. What might an employer be interested in? Again, take a moment and make a list of what interests your potential employer may have.

They might value things like the following:

- Avoiding the cost of churn and replacing staff by having employees who are likely to stay a long time.
- Having employees who want to learn more so their skills grow and change with a changing competitive environment.
- Growing the next generation of our company's leaders with staff members who show initiative and want to take on more responsibility.
- Having staff who are willing to move from place to place and who are culturally competent to meet global needs.

Perhaps you have come up with your own similar ideas, or others. The idea is to step into their shoes and try to figure out what is likely to be important to them. As in the case of salary, you should do some research about this beforehand. Virtually every company has on-line literature such as annual reports, advertisements, and personnel ads that will tell you a ton about their hopes, dreams, and strategies—and yes, their interests. There may also be recent stories in newspapers and trade journals that will be of value. Take the time to read these things. An hour or two spent doing this will pay huge dividends. Also, talk to friends you know in the firm. Yes, that's allowed!

You can also use the negotiating session itself to tease out some of the company's interests. Let's see how Pat, a potential employee, handles this.

The sequence here is especially important.

Employer: Pat, we are so pleased about the possibility of your joining us. I'd like to talk about your salary today.

Pat: Oh, thank you. Before we do that, though, I have a few questions about some things that might be important to both of us.

Employer: Like what?

Pat: Well, I am really excited about this company and its future, and I would like to be part of that. In particular, over time, I have an interest in learning about other aspects of the company so that I might be able to contribute in different roles as the years go by. Do you have a program or an approach that would help me learn things outside of my initial job responsibilities?

Employer: I am really pleased to hear you ask that. We have a great interest in growing our own. But my department is pretty small, and we don't have many resources for such things.

Pat: Perhaps the company has a program that it offers more broadly?

Employer: Oh, yes. You just reminded me. The corporation just instituted a management training program for selected staff members who have interests like yours. Each month, they take two to three days off from their regular job and rotate through the company. There are also special lectures and training exercises that the company pays for. Then, you are given two to three month assignments in different parts of the company.

Pat: Wow, that sounds great. How could we make sure that I am eligible for that program?

Employer: Part of the deal is that you may have to be flexible in where you work, as this firm has operations throughout the country.

Pat: I have always had a great interest in travel and learning about other parts of the world, so that would be very attractive to me.

Employer: Good. Let me work with our administrative folks to make sure that is part of your offer letter.

Get it? Remember that we talked about sequence? This is a great kind of conversation to have before you talk about money. In so doing, you are actively making the employer even more keen to have you as a staff member. Why? Because you have demonstrated empathy with the company's underlying interests. You have also shown that your interests are congruent with their own.

By the way, that commonality of interests may prove helpful if and when you pursue the dollar issue in a later part of the conversation. The interest-based negotiation can be integrated into the salary-specific part of the talk. Let's say it looks like Pat isn't going to get the hoped-for starting salary. He asked about a signing bonus, and that doesn't look good either. He still really likes many things about the company and the job, though, and is willing to forego income for a time if he has a reasonable chance of making more later. This is one approach:

Pat: Well, I am a little disappointed on the money front, but let's explore other ideas that might help make this work. How often would I expect a performance and salary review?

Employer: The standard approach is an annual review.

Pat: What are the possibilities, if I participate in that training program we discussed, that I would have a chance for earlier or more frequent salary reviews?

Employer: Well, I'd have to ask about that and get back to you.

Pat: Please explain to folks that I am really just asking for the expedited review. I understand that you cannot commit, at this time, to a specific salary increase with each review. After all, I would have to show that I deserved that. If I deserve an increase, fine. If not, I'll trust your judgment and try to make sure I do deserve it the next time!

Employer: That seems very reasonable to me. Let me check it with our folks.

Note that Pat did not frame this portion of the conversation as a diatribe about why the money offer was inadequate. He did not engage in positional bargaining: "I need and demand $85,000 per year." Instead he adopted a more thoughtful approach, one concerned with the full set of his interests and that of the employer.

So, he didn't get the money, yet, but he has started to create a mechanism that will help satisfy his interest in earning more money over time. Maybe Pat has asked for something a bit out of the ordinary, but it is in the context of helping the company to satisfy its interest in providing advancement opportunities for its staff. Pat has also made it easy for them to say yes, in that they are committing only to a process, not a specific result. Further, the person with whom Pat is negotiating has now taken on the role of Pat's advocate with other people in the company.

Interests are interesting

Not all interests are highly quantifiable. Some are tangible and some are intangible. Some are subjective and some are objective. For example, money is tangible and amounts of money are objective, but the process by which you achieve wealth might be more intangible and subjective. Nonetheless, you want to assess and prioritize the full set of your interests, and at the same time you also want to try to understand the same on the part of your employer.

Then, you want to meld the two sets of interests into a workable package. How do you do it?

One way is to think long-term rather than in the short-term. Pat was doing this in the discussion above. He was trying to satisfy his interests by creating a multi-month or multi-year process that would lead to a better financial result for him, while also being attentive to the company's interest in not paying him more than he was worth. The actual number of dollars that will emerge from this process cannot be known for some time, but the creation of a timeline for the process is something consistent with the interests of both parties. Pat even tossed some humor in to emphasize the point: *If I deserve an increase, fine. If not, I'll trust your judgment and try to make sure I do deserve it the next time!*

Sometimes, we need to bring in outside resources to help satisfy the parties' interests. Again Pat's prospective deal does this. Recall that the management training program was not offered by the particular department of the company for which Pat will work. It is a resource offered by the central administration of the company. You can't tell just from the dialogue we have presented, but Pat had actually learned about this program in one of the corporation's on-line publications during his pre-negotiation research. So, he was prepared to suggest the use of this outside resource to help satisfy both parties' interests.

Inventing Options

Sometimes you have to invent options as part of satisfying each party's interests. That process of invention can be pretty exciting and fun if you approach it in a positive way. Be alert, though, to the fact that you may have to be explicit with the other party on the process of inventing options. Let's go back to Pat:

Pat: I have ideas about some other areas that I would like to explore. I think they are quite consistent with where the company is headed and its interests, but I am not sure how we might satisfy them. Do you mind if we do a little brainstorming?

Employer: I am intrigued. What do you have in mind?

Pat: Well, I have often found that if we spend a few minutes creatively thinking about options, we can come up with a bunch of them. We can then critique them. Some will be infeasible, and some will be good. The idea is that we both make suggestions with the understanding that neither of us "owns" any idea.

Employer: Can you be more specific?

Pat: Yes, I would like to get advanced training in a different field from my undergraduate work. In particular, I want to learn Mandarin. That kind of language development would help me broaden my horizons and perspective, something I really care about. I think your company also wants to have staff members who bring a broad perspective and an ability to communicate with customers around the world, and China is the world's biggest market.

Employer: But we don't have a foreign language program here.

Pat: I know, and I wouldn't expect you to. Here's where the brainstorming comes in. Let's spend just a few minutes inventing ways I, and perhaps others, could learn Mandarin. After we come up with a list, we can evaluate the ideas and see if any make sense. No obligations, just an exploration. I'll keep track on this white board as we go along.

Employer: Ok, I am intrigued!

Ten minutes later.

Employer: You know, that idea of asking native Mandarin speakers to start a lunchtime club to teach interested staff the language is a good one. It would be good for team-building. It might also help those staffers improve their English, as well!

Pat: And if we combine it with the idea of after-work social events in Chinatown, going to restaurants and concerts, it will be even better.

Employer: And I bet I can get the HR department to buy into the idea of paying for training manuals to supplement the lunch clubs. Maybe they can also follow up on the idea of getting the college next door to invite our language students to Mandarin events over there.

Pat: Wow, it looks like we have invented a whole package that could be really awesome!

Employer: Let's go for it!

During a brainstorming session, it is important that you defer criticism while you are developing options. Afterwards, it is time to analyze the ideas. Here are the kinds of questions you want to ask afterwards while trying to see if the ideas will satisfy both parties' interests.

- Why?
- Why not?
- How have other people solved this problem?
- How might we relax some of the constraints?
- Who else might we need to involve?

We are betting this sounds pretty involved. You are probably wondering how it will be received by the employer. Well, a lot depends on how you present it. This is something you might want to practice at home with a friend. But, even if you don't have time to practice, if you are friendly, open, and respectful, most employers will be tremendously impressed with your thoughtfulness and maturity. Remember that you and your employer are each making an investment in a future together, and this conversation is just one continuing part of establishing a longer-term relationship. If you frame it this way, you can think about the conversation as a way to explore how each party will invest in the other – and you will set the stage for the kinds of conversations and explorations that will be useful to you in your day to day work. They will want you even more to join their company.

Let's summarize the major steps to enhance the possibility of productive interest-based negotiation:

1. The point of a negotiation is to satisfy the full set of the parties' interests, tangible and intangible, objective and subjective.

2. Avoid positional bargaining.

3. Away from the table: Think about your interests and write them down.

4. Away from the table: Conduct research on the other party's interests.

5. At the table: Continue to learn about the company's interests.

6. At the table: Invent, perhaps through brainstorming, ways of satisfying both parties' interests.

7. At the table: Create a workable package of elements that, in combination, satisfies both

parties' interests.

You are making good progress, but now you need the secret sauce that makes this all work:

Trading on differences.

STEP 6:

Trade on Differences

Mark Twain said, "It is not best that we should all think alike; *it is difference of opinion that makes horse races.*" What did he mean? He was suggesting that two people looking at the same group of horses and jockeys would predict differently which one would win. If we consider that people often bet on horse races, he was saying that people assign a different monetary value to the same thing.

This simple observation has great power in a negotiation if you are alert enough to apply it wisely. The power is that the application of this principle can transform a negotiation from one in which the two parties "split the pie" —if I get more, you get less—to one in which there are joint gains. The pie is actually made larger, and we *both* do better than if we had not come to an agreement. Most people think of differences as separating us. In negotiation, differences have the power to make a deal possible.

Thinking about the world in this manner is hard to do as it requires a change in the traditional mindset. Our colleague, Harvard Business School Professor Jim Sebenius, points out that there is a powerful tendency to see negotiations as mainly "zero-sum" or "win-lose:" If I get more you end up with less. He notes that this tendency comes from a psychological phenomenon known as "incompatibility bias." People tend to see the other party's interests as strictly opposed to their own, leading to a "mythical fixed-pie" view. The result is that competitive moves by each individual to claim value in a negotiation often drive out the cooperative moves that could create value and realize joint gains.

Let us again illustrate with a true story provided by negotiation expert David Lax. Several years ago, people at General Motors were facing competitive pressures from around the world. They went to their local electric utility company, Detroit Edison. "The electricity rates you charge us are too high," was the complaint, "making it hard for us to compete against car manufacturers in regions with lower energy costs. We need you to lower your rates."

The folks at the electric utility replied, "We can't do that. Our rates are regulated by the state. Besides, if we lowered our rates for you, we would have to do it for others, too, since the law prohibits price discrimination."

"That's your problem," said the GM people. "If you can't lower our rates, we will shift our manufacturing to Tennessee or another state with lower energy costs."

Since you are now an expert at positional versus interest-based negotiation, you have recognized that both parties were at risk of being trapped by their words. Luckily, the folks at the utility company were perceptive enough to see that GM's interest was in lowering its production costs. Although the auto company was complaining about electricity rates, any kind of cost reduction would be helpful. The utility people also understood about trading on differences.

"What if we were to think about the following," they posited. "You use several million tons of coal in your factories for heating your plants. We use billions of tons in our power plants to generate electricity. With our buying power, we get a much better price per ton than you. What if we were to become your coal purchasing agent, selling coal to you at a substantial discount from what you pay now?"

"Further, you have several dozen electrical transformers in your manufacturing plant. We have several million in our service territory. With our purchasing power and technical staff, we are able to buy and maintain transformers at a much lower cost than you. What if we were to become your purchasing and maintenance service company for transformers?"

As Lax reports, the deal was quickly done. The rates charged for electricity stayed the same, but GM was able to achieve substantial economies by letting Detroit Edison use its expertise in service to its customer. Indeed, Detroit Edison actually made a bit of extra money with its fuel and supply service contracts. The pie grew. Both parties came out ahead.

Let's analyze this a bit. What were the "horses" in this race that had different value to the two parties? Coal and transformers. GM was essentially a retail purchaser of these production inputs, paying a relatively high price in the marketplace. Detroit Edison's scale meant that it was a wholesale purchaser, getting the advantage of lower prices through bulk purchases. The coal and the transformers were still coal and transformers, but the two parties valued them differently because of their particular circumstances.

Having Detroit Edison provide the coal and transformers had a high value to the auto company but could be done at a low cost to Detroit Edison.

The Detroit Edison negotiators helped the GM people make an inventory of these differences, and then the parties were able to trade on the differences. The resulting deal was better for both parties than if they had never gotten together. And it was certainly a better result than if the parties had stuck to their original positions.

There are lots of possibilities for how the same item or commodity can be viewed differently by two parties to a negotiation. For example, people often have different time preferences. For one person, $1000 received in six months is just as good as $1000 received today because he doesn't have many real options to get a high return on the money during that period. For another person, that $1000 six months from now is worth a lot less than it would be today because she has an opportunity to earn a really high interest rate on it. We call this a difference in time preference based on implicit discount rates.

Other people view the same item differently because they have alternate views of the future. If I were to offer to sell you a voucher for 1000 gallons of gasoline for a firm price of $4 per gallon in five years, you might be reluctant to accept because you think the price is going down to $3. We have a different forecast. To reach a negotiation that trades on this difference, we might enter into a contingent contract, where the number of gallons you get in five years is dependent on the change in the consumer price index. I will make sure that the formula we use still gives me a bit of a profit, and you will make sure that it holds you harmless to overall price changes in the economy. We both

come out ahead. We call this a difference based on fore-
casts, probabilities, and beliefs.

To start to bring this concept home for the purposes of
this book, we might also have a different view of someone's
motivation. You are about to be hired and the employer
assumes that you are about as motivated as the average
new staffer. You know, though, that you are incredibly self-
directed and ambitious. You start off asking for more
money, but since the employer can't yet be sure that you
are worth it, they say "no." You respond by saying, "What
if we were to agree on a bonus plan that rewards me if I
exceed your expectations in bringing value to the firm?"

Here, the employer can agree. If you do bring that
extra value, it is well worth their while to pay you for it.
If you do not, they don't have to pay out that additional
money. When "the ingredient" we trade on is a different
perception of motivation, "the recipe" for joint gains is an
incentive-based contract.

Find alternative value

When you trade on differences, you want to find things
that arc of high value to you, but low cost to your new
employer, or vice versa. It makes it easy for them to say
"yes," and the different valuation thereby makes a deal possible.

Here's another example of a potential trade on differences: Virtually all US employers offer health insurance as
an employee benefit. When they offer you a salary, they are
implicitly adding in this cost as part of the offer. They need
to account for the health insurance in this way because
they have to make sure their overall cost of keeping you
on as a staff member is within their budget. But you may

have a different view of the value of that health insurance. For example, your spouse may already have family coverage with another employer. Or, if you are not married, maybe you can be covered under your parents' health insurance plan for several more years. There is thus no need for you to have a health insurance policy at your new job. This situation creates a difference upon which you can trade. You might say, "I can forego having the company provide health insurance to me. What if we were to apply a portion of the cost you otherwise would incur to my base salary?"

Here, the insurance is of low value to you but of high cost to the employer. You've offered to share the savings generated by your willingness to forego a standard benefit offered by the employer. The negotiated result is a higher salary for you and a lower cost of business for the company. The pie has been made bigger and then split so there are gains for both parties.

Here's something else that might work for you under certain conditions:

When someone is hired as a full-time staff member in the US, a company has to incur certain tax expenses, contributing to Social Security and the unemployment fund and Medicare. When someone is hired as a consultant, the company does not have these obligations. Also, if you work as a consultant, you may be able to deduct several types of expenses related to your work (e.g., home office, computers, travel, etc.) If you are willing to be a consultant, you are able to offer a deal that trades on these differences in tax treatment. Specifically, you can often obtain a higher daily rate than would have been the case as a staff member. Again, if you can reach an agreement on this, both you and the company can come out ahead.[1]

An important thing to remember is that a trade on differences can often involve a series of events and results that unfold over time. It is therefore imperative to make sure the details are defined. With items such as a negotiated agreement that includes performance bonuses, make sure the mechanism is agreed to in advance and put into the negotiated agreement. There's nothing worse than waiting a year and having a disagreement about what performance metrics are going to be used to determine your bonus. You want to do your best to capture the shared interests in the design of the agreement—based on objective criteria—so there are no squabbles or misunderstandings. If you specify the agreement properly and carefully, the execution of that design is automatic and without controversy.

It will be helpful to think ahead of time about what differences you can trade on. This comes from being clear about your interests and that of the company. You can turn back to the lists you made as you defined interests in the last step and do some more research. But let's think about this strategically. As we discussed, you want to have learned a lot about the interests of your employer. How is the company doing? Look at their employment statistics and see how fast they are growing. Where are they facing challenges and constraints? What are their hopes, in terms of market growth and new lines of business? All of this information is there for you to find from publicly available sources. A fast growing company might place a high val-

---

1 Do your research carefully here. As a consultant, you will have to pay self-employment tax, and you want to be sure you have fully accounted for that and other tax issues. Also, the company has to be sure that you meet the legal definition of a consultant, or they can get into trouble with the government.

ue on an employee's willingness to move. Such flexibility could be of low cost to you if you don't care about where you live. A smaller company might value employees who are willing to work long hours and take on broad responsibilities. That extra work may be of low cost to you if you have the time to spare and want to gain a broad range of experience.

You want to understand your interests very well, too. For example, don't sign an incentive-based contract if you really need to know how much money you are going to make every year. Don't offer to forego health insurance if your spouse might be leaving his or her job in a few months. Don't offer to be a consultant if you really need employer-based benefits or don't have the inclination to learn the ins and outs of running your own small enterprise.

Learn at the table

Although we have emphasized the need to do prenegotiation research about the employer's interests, you should also look for opportunities to learn more about those interests as the discussion proceeds at the table. After all, not all information is presented in public documents and other materials. The person at the table is a font of insights about the status of their company and other valuable facts. So, ask questions.

Beyond asking questions, we'd like to suggest that you engage in what psychologists call "active listening." Active listening is characterized by playing back to the person something that she has just said. This technique will bring you surprises because we tend to be really bad listeners, especially in stressful situations. Sometimes we actually hear the opposite of what people have said because we are so busy thinking about the next thing we are going to say. For example, an active listener might say, "Oh, did I understand you to mean that the company is serious about penetrating the Chinese market?" The response might be, "No, I said that we can't seriously think about penetrating the Chinese market." The reply, "Oh, thanks for clearing up my misunderstanding."

You can also use the opportunity of the negotiating session to understand your own interests better. Be modest about what you know about yourself. You are early to the job market and just starting your career. There may be a number of things that are presented by the employer that teach you something about yourself. Be open to that.

After you have a good understanding of their interests and yours, make a "Differences Inventory." What aspects of the job might present a different valuation for you and the company? As we have mentioned, you are looking for things that have a high value to one party and a low cost to the other. Jointly explore with the employer how you might trade on those differences. Remember to say "What if?" rather than asking a "yes-no" question. When you find that joint gains are possible, codify the method for achieving those gains in writing as part of your deal.

As you think through trading on differences, keep in mind:

1. People often put a different value on the same commodity, object, or result.
2. When there is a difference in perceived value—high value to one party and low cost to the other—it is possible to trade on differences.

3. Trading on differences can produce joint gains, "expanding the pie."

4. To trade on differences:

Away from the table

• Conduct research on the other party's interests.

• Think about your own interests.

• Construct a differences inventory.

At the table

• Continue to learn about the company's interests and your own.

• Jointly explore how you might trade on those differences.

• Codify the methods that will be used to achieve the joint gains.

Real Life Story: Rebecca

When Rebecca first took on a position managing an international program at a university, the initial salary offer was far below what she was making at her current position in the non-profit world. However, she was very interested in the job and knew that it would provide a springboard for work she wanted to do in the future. The offer had been made after an extensive committee interview process involving several members of the faculty and administration, so Rebecca was confident that they thought she was the right candidate for the job and were anxious to close the deal. The university's hiring scales, however, were quite inflexible. Despite a concerted effort to move the needle on base salary, she and her hiring manager had hit a ceiling. They agreed to meet for a cup of coffee to see if they could explore options to improve the deal.

Rebecca opened the conversation by saying:

"Thanks for meeting with me to talk things over, Martha. I'm really interested in working with you and your team to help build this new program, and meeting everyone over the last several weeks has made me even more interested in coming on board. Thanks for your help in getting the starting salary adjusted from the initial offer. As you know, there's still a substantial gap between what is being offered, my current salary, and our joint expectations for this role. I wonder if we could think together about some creative ways to resolve this difference. For instance, perhaps we could agree that whenever I need to fly to India, I could travel through Heathrow airport and visit my family in London. There would be no additional cost to the program if I were to do that, and it would mean a lot to me."

"Of course," said Martha, "That's easy, and it would be entirely fine with me if you were to do that. In fact, if you'd like to spend a few days there en route and work remotely, that would be fine, too."

"That sounds great," said Rebecca. "I can't wait to get to work. When can I start?"

What happened here? Stopping off in London was of high value to Rebecca but of low cost to Martha. By trading on that difference, they were able to craft a deal at little cost to the employer that helped overcome what might have been a deal-breaking deadlock on salary.

STEP 7:

Sharpen Your Tactics

Anchors Away

Here's a question we often ask our negotiation pupils: "Whether you are engaged in buying or selling, should you offer a price first or wait for the other person to do so?"

Most often, people tell us that they would rather wait for the other person to suggest a price. They point out that letting the other person go first provides information to them about the other party's BATNA and interests. While that is true, letting them make the first offer may not be the correct answer. Whether you are buying or selling, it can be best for you to be the first to offer a price.

The theory behind this conclusion, supported by tons of empirical evidence, is that the first price on the table acts as an anchor to the negotiation. As our colleague David Lax likes to say, an anchor is like an X-ray, invisible but powerful. It acts to skew the ultimate conclusion of the negotiation towards the number offered.

The striking thing about anchoring is that there does

not have to be substantive support for an anchor to take hold. In their book, *The Manager as Negotiator*, Lax and Jim Sebenius relate an experiment that demonstrates this:

> *[I]n one experiment, groups of college students were asked to name the percentage of the countries in the United Nations that are African. Before answering the question, a roulette wheel (modified to have the numbers one through one hundred) was spun in front of the students. For one typical group, the wheel stopped at 10 percent; for another group it landed at 65 percent. The first group was asked if the percentage of U.N. nations that are African was higher or lower than 10 percent ... ; the other group was asked whether the percentage was higher or lower than 65 percent ... Surprisingly, the first group's estimate were strikingly lower than those of the second: the mean of the first group's estimates was 24 percent while the mean of the second group's estimate was 45 percent! Thus, the clearly irrelevant piece of information—a randomly chosen starting point of 10 percent versus 65 percent—seemed strongly to anchor their perceptions about the proportion of U.N. member nations that are African.*

The advantages inherent in making the first offer, though, are not without limit. The effectiveness of your offer as an anchor is dramatically reduced if it is clearly outside of a zone of reasonableness. In fact, if you anchor too high, you might just be perceived as greedy and out of touch with the employer's business needs. Here's where pre-negotiation research comes into play. Just as you would check the Blue Book value before anchoring someone with a price for a car purchase, you should consult available sources of information to find a reasonable range of salaries for the job you are discussing.

What if the other person drops his anchor before you have a chance? It has been shown often that the final result of a negotiation is often halfway between the original anchor and the response offered by the other party, provided of course that the midpoint lies within the ZOPA, the zone of possible agreement. Accordingly, your response to an initial offer when you have been anchored, note Lax and Sebenius, "should be chosen so that the midpoint between the two offers is at the negotiator's [i.e., your] aspiration level."

The point we are making here is that you want to think explicitly about the pros and cons of anchoring before you get to the table. If you make the first offer, you may influence the results of the negotiations in ways you find attractive. On the other hand, if you let them make the first offer, you will gain valuable information, but then you might have to think carefully about how to "re-anchor" the discussion. There is no right or wrong answer here. We'd just like you to be prepared one way or the other.

Handling the questions you don't want to answer

Some of the most unsettling moments in a negotiation occur when the other party asks you a question you really don't want to answer. Certain questions can put you in a tough spot; for example, "What's your real bottom line?" You don't want to lie, but if you answer truthfully, you can be squeezed. Sometimes, too, the person asking the question truly has no right to the answer he or she seeks. An uncomfortable choice awaits you. Should you answer honestly, or should you hedge, or should you decline to answer?

This concept of anticipating and dealing with difficult questions—the ones you hope you don't have to tackle—is an emerging area of research within the negotiation community. Our colleague Jim Sebenius, who directed Harvard Business School's negotiation unit for many years, has done an extensive amount of research on this tricky topic. Jim helps us think about some types of hard   questions we might face, and he offers possible answers that he has seen in the business world. We spoke with him and have paraphrased and consolidated some of his ideas.

Let's explore some possible questions you might encounter during a job negotiation:

Question: What's the least you are willing to take as a salary?

Possible answer: I hope and believe that both of us are looking to settle on a salary that is competitive in the marketplace and commensurate with my abilities and the responsibilities of the job. I have told you what amount seems right to me and have told you the reasons. If you have a different view of the right number, please let me know and explain the reasons.

Question: With whom else are you negotiating?

Possible answer: I view my negotiations with you as confidential. Likewise, I must keep any other negotiations confidential.

Question: I'm trying to gauge your real level of interest and commitment to this job and our company. If I were to offer you this job right now with the basic terms of salary, etc., as we have discussed, would you definitely accept it?

Yes or no?

Possible answer: This is a big decision for me, in terms of where I hope to spend the next few years of my career, and I need some time to think it over. Please let me know the date by which you must have my final answer.

Question: This is my final offer. Take it or leave it. I need your answer immediately. What will it be?

Possible answer: I'm afraid I'll have to walk away. I don't want to, but the offer doesn't quite meet my needs. I'd like to have one more attempt to find a way through—let's take one more stab at figuring out a creative solution that would work for both of us. However, if this is your final word, I understand and respect your decision.

Question: Don't you trust me?

Possible answer: I don't see this as an issue of trust between you and me. This is about a multi-year agreement between me and the company, and I fully intend to carry out my commitments and have no reason to believe that the company would not do the same.

Let's think through the characteristics of these answers.

First, they are respectful. Second, they are honest. Sometimes, the respondent has to do a bit of shuffling or ju-jitsu to avoid a direct answer, but he is careful to not give the questioner information to which he or she has no right.

Thinking in advance about the hardest questions you might be asked and how you will answer them is good practice in and of itself. There is an additional benefit, though. Thinking through your possible answers will actually help you better understand your BATNA and your interests. Look again at the sample answers given above. Notice how much more confident you can be in your answers if you have considered your alternatives to the job being discussed. Likewise, if you have thought about what really matters to you. (By the way, preparing for this kind of question really isn't so different from preparing for tricky questions you might encounter in the interview process. Just as you might think in advance about and rehearse your response to a possible question from an interviewer about a time that you failed, for example, a little bit of forethought and preparation in this particular vein will put you in good stead.)

Finally, we suggest that you actually practice out loud answering the hardest questions. Ask a friend to ask you the questions and answer them. You'll find that certain words and phrases are awkward, and so it might take several tries to get your answer down pat. Then, if and when the questions come up in your job negotiation, answering them will feel natural.

Avoiding a personal pitfall

Many first time job negotiators make the mistake of bringing up the cost of their student loan payments or rent to justify asking for a higher salary figure. These numbers are neither compelling nor relevant. An employer doesn't care if you worked your way through college while supporting your siblings, have just bought your own condo, or want to live in a fashionable downtown location. As we have suggested, employers base their salary offers on what a position is worth, so stick to talking about factors that are related to the responsibilities you will take on. Use what you have learned about salary ranges in the market place. Then, focus on the value of competencies that you bring—or might bring, with some training and mentoring —to the company's long-term vision.

Real life Story: Steven

Sometimes people assume that an employer won't be able to budge on salary, so they jump right away to looking for more creative currency. This happened to our friend Steven when he accepted a faculty position at a university in Australia.

Steven was an attractive candidate—he had just graduated with a PhD from Stanford, considered to have the best program in his field of study. His dissertation work and research interests were directly related to a program that the university wanted to grow, and the university was conducting an international search. Because Steven had gone to graduate school after several years in the work world, he also had a valuable set of professional connections and practical experience that set him apart from many candidates. Yet, when the university made him an offer—which was a good one, consistent with starting salaries for other junior faculty—he assumed they had put together the best financial package they could. After all, they were trying to woo him to make a move with his family.

As Steven noted, "When the university made me an offer, I hesitantly asked if I couldn't get more travel funds. They said no because that number is set centrally university-wide, so I said okay and accepted the offer. I later learned that they were so eager to get me that I could have 'asked for anything' salary-wise."

Steven made a classic mistake. He did his background research on salaries and the like. He started to explore if there was room to trade further on differences. But, when he hit an obstacle, he stopped. He hadn't asked enough questions to understand how far the university was willing to go to make him happy, and he effectively under-asked.

STEP 8:

Practice

You know your BATNA, you have a good sense of the ZOPA and how you might try to influence an employer's perceptions of it. You're prepared with your list of your own interests and the company's interests, and you've thought about the hardest question you are likely to face. But are you really ready?

Now that you have all of this material, you can benefit from trying it out. Rehearse what you want to say. The more you repeat your questions and your statements, the more natural they will become to you and the more comfortable you will be when you head into negotiations.

Find someone who will rehearse with you. Explain to them the parameters and then do some improvisation. Tell your rehearsal partner to ask you the tough questions and maybe add in a couple of unexpected ones. This will help you think through your answers before you are put on the spot.

But beyond a formal rehearsal, use the rest of your life—in school, with your family, in social situations—

to try to enhance some of the skills that will benefit you in all relationships. Start with active listening: Really pay attention to and hear what people you meet with are saying. Ask them questions that will show you have heard them and clarify what they meant.

You can also work on building trusting relationships. Take some time in talking with people you have just met. Ask them about themselves and find a connection with them. It is less threatening to do this when you are not about to launch into a negotiation, and it will prepare you for when you are.

Pay more attention to and take more control over the negotiations you face every day. Some of them are obvious such as when you rent an apartment, buy a used mobile phone or sign up for television service. Some are less clear—buying shoes at a retail store, figuring out who is going to do the dishes, or deciding what movie to go see.

In these interactions, you can find ways to trade on differences, to increase the size of the pie and then to split it so that everyone is more satisfied. Doing this with the transactions you are used to will give you the confidence to do so when it comes to the job that will dictate much of your future.

Our friend Zahra told us about how she overcame her initial discomfort with negotiating. She would go out of her way to find opportunities where she could practice in low-risk situations. She started out getting comfortable with the art of basic haggling—going to flea auctions and farmers markets, striking up conversations with purveyors about their wares. She soon found that she had begun to enjoy the process of getting to know something about someone and why they were selling or making a particular product. And, she discovered that when she approached settling on a price in that manner, she and the purveyor both enjoyed the process more—and, she usually got a better price.

As Zahra got more comfortable from approaching negotiations in this manner, she tried out increasingly complex deals. Now, she says, she is much more confident in her ability to step into a negotiating situation and help craft conversation that creates value for both sides.

On the Issue of Gender

Are women worse negotiators than men? A number of studies indicate that there are differences in both approach and response.

As the next generation moving into the marketplace and as individuals who are making decisions about your own careers, you should consider the implications of these studies both for yourselves and for your future workplace.

The lack of negotiating success on the part of women can breed resentment and slow down the career paths of women relative to men. There is a lot of evidence for these conclusions, and it transcends all fields and all levels, from women just starting their careers to accomplished women running Fortune 500 companies.

Women are attending college at higher rates than men, graduating in greater numbers and earning higher grades. Yet one year after graduation, women were making only 82 percent of what their male colleagues were paid, according to a 2012 report, "Graduating to a Pay Gap," from the American Association of University Women.

Even when men and women had the same majors, there were often gaps in pay. The researchers found that female business majors earned an average of slightly more than $38,000, while men earned just over $45,000. In engineering, technology, computer science and social sciences fields, researchers found that women made between 77 percent and 88 percent of what their male colleagues were paid.

"This pay gap is not merely the result of women's choices," researchers Christianne Corbett and Catherine Hill wrote in the pay gap report. "Lower earnings have an immediate effect after college, setting into motion a chain of disparities that will follow women throughout their careers."

There are indications that the wage gap is not just about the careers that women are choosing. It's about how they are negotiating and that they may be penalized if they do.

In a study by Professor Linda Babcock at Carnegie Mellon, men and women asked for raises using identical scripts. People liked the men's style, but the women were branded as aggressive—unless they gave a smile while they asked, or appeared warm and friendly. In other words, unless they conformed to feminine stereotypes.

"The data shows that men are able to negotiate for themselves without facing any negative consequences, but when women negotiate, people often like them less and want to work with them less," says Sheryl Sandberg, Facebook's chief operating officer, whose book *Lean In* is about women and leadership. "Even if women haven't studied this or seen this data, they often implicitly understand this, so they hold back."

It's not an issue limited to America.

Dr. Yasmin Davidds, leader of Women's Institute of Negotiation, interviewed 700 women from 22 countries who had recently completed a top negotiation training program. While all of them had learned how to negotiate, less than 40 percent were using their new skills in every day negotiations, compared to 98 percent of their male counterparts.

Davidds commented:

"It was clear that learning the skills, strategies and techniques of negotiation was not enough for women and only one part of the equation, the second and most critical part was working with their subconscious—the part that holds disempowering beliefs about what they feel they deserve."

The danger of following the rules

Women often feel that if they follow "the rules," they will be treated well.

Our colleague Brenda Curiel put it this way:

"Part of what has been difficult for me to ask for what I actually think my value might be may be hardwired as a woman or it might be part of my conditioning, but I have a deep sense of asking being boorish and if I'm truly making contributions, a big daddy will pat me on the head and say "well done" and offer me a commensurate reward. If that isn't happening, well, I should just work harder and be better and then it will!"

Authors Jodi Detjen, Michelle Waters, and Kelly Watson elaborate on this in their book *The Orange Line*.

"Our book talks about why women don't negotiate

because they make two assumptions. First, tangible, material rewards are not supposed to be important because we are 'nice' and, second, if we follow the rules, good things will happen because we are 'nice.'"

Linda Babcock and Sara Laschever address this in their book, *Women Don't Ask*. They conclude that women don't like to negotiate:

- In surveys, 2.5 times more women than men said they feel "a great deal of apprehension" about negotiating.

- Men initiate negotiations about four times as often as women.

- When asked to pick metaphors for the process of negotiating, men picked "winning a ballgame" and a "wrestling match," while women picked "going to the dentist."

- Women will pay as much as $1,353 to avoid negotiating the price of a car, which may help explain why 63 percent of Saturn car buyers are women.

- Women are more pessimistic about how much is available when they do negotiate and so they typically ask for and get less when they do negotiate—on average, 30 percent less than men.

- 20 percent of adult women (22 million people) say they never negotiate at all, even though they often recognize negotiation as appropriate and even necessary.

But what do we do about the facts noted above by Professor Babcock? As repeated by Evelyn Murphy, former Lt. Gov. of Massachusetts, "Women are perceived differently," and can face backlash when they negotiate hard. Evelyn talks about the importance of understanding the mechanics of negotiation, but also stresses the need for women to have the self-confidence to negotiate in an effective way. "A lot of this has to do with one's mindset. We have to understand the relational equation, to understand what it takes to be effective in our own styles and voices."

Victoria Budson, executive director of the Women and Public Policy Program at Harvard's Kennedy School of Government and chair of the Massachusetts Commission on the Status of Women, expands by noting that if women appear more relational in the discussion, they do better in terms of the results achieved. "They have to signal more relationally than their male counterparts to be heard the same."

We take this a step further, after hearing comments from Sheila English, an accomplished businesswoman and public administrator. Sheila urges women—for the sake of their own comfort in the negotiation—to rely on the same kind of interpersonal skills with which they are most comfortable in the rest of their lives. Rather than trying to enter the negotiation in a "male style"—all business, assertive, and direct from the get-go—spend time working on building a relationship with the hiring representative. In other words, play to your natural inclinations.

Imagine this kind of approach in your meeting with the hiring manager:

Employer: We're pleased to offer you this job at a starting salary of $xx, health care benefits [and so on.]

You: Thank you so much. I'm honored and pleased. Before we talk about the details of your offer, I was wondering if you could tell me a bit about yourself. As you know, I'm new to the job market, and it would really help me get a perspective on things. How long have you been here? What kind of jobs did you have before this one?

Back-and-forth discussion, with questions from you like: "What have you found you like best about working here?" "Have you found you have created strong relationships with your colleagues?"

Then, when the time is ripe, dive into the offer details and negotiation using the strategies and techniques we've suggested. We think you will be more comfortable in "your own skin." And, as noted by Murphy and Budson, we think you will be less likely to provoke hostile responses.

While relational signals are clearly important, please also be prepared on the substantive side of things. Joyce Murphy, an accomplished state government, hospital, and university administrator, offers her insights:

"The best advice I can provide is for women to do their homework and to know their value! It is so much easier today to get salary and market information than when I was starting out but there were still even then opportunities to research salary levels for positions. I advise young women that it is important to know what you want, in concert with what the market intelligence provides and to be thinking about other benefits that are important to you and that you may be willing or interested in negotiating in addition to salary. In fact, there may be some things that are more important than salary but women need not compromise too much on the financial end. Again, being prepared for the discussion, having done the homework and having received some coaching/confidence building prior to that conversation all contribute to a successful negotiation."

Find the style and approach and support that works for you.

Jessica Boatright, an accomplished public government and non-profit administrator, explains her approach to keeping on target with regard to her aspirations:

"I think one thing that is especially important for young women is to psyche themselves up for a negotiation. Before negotiating a salary, pick a few older people that you respect who've had jobs in your industry and talk to them specifically about the negotiation process, what to expect, and what they've found to be successful. (Pick someone from both genders.) Read a few articles about women and negotiating the day before your conversation. And then put a little bird on your shoulder—the "would a man accept this offer" bird, and then try to use that for encouragement during the conversation. I am serious: I try to bring that imaginary bird with me, and sometimes she helps."

In contrast, our friend Brenda, mentioned above, adopts a highly quantitative approach:

"When I have addressed this issue, and I actually have often, I have prepared heavily. I have run all kinds of mini (and sometimes major) financial models that justify the package I am proposing with future value predictions and almost at-risk type performance guarantees."

You might not want to dive so far into the math as Brenda! But, look at her final thought on the matter. Notwithstanding her research, she, like Jessica, still feels a need to invent a way to get past her personal reluctance to bargain hard for herself.

"If I can get my head into the place that I am negotiating a contract for the product/service that is Brenda vs.

me asking for a little bit more "just because," then I'm quite confident and have been very successful."

You can be successful, too, if you think about and employ the excellent advice offered by these thoughtful and accomplished women.

Final Words

Every negotiation will hit a limit at some stage or the other. As we recommended earlier, try to keep track of how the process is going by employing Bill Ury's stance of "standing on the balcony."

Be mindful of both direct indications and indirect non-verbal signals from your counterpart. A firm may simply not be able to do any more for you. You need to have the grace and presence at that stage to decide whether to accept the final offer on the table, or walk away. Knowing your BATNA and practicing the negotiation skills we have laid out for you will help you understand when and how to do that. But we'd like to leave you with a final thought.

Don't feel pressure when an employer tries to back you into a "take-it-or-leave-it" situation. An employer may try to convince you that you are so lucky to have a job or a chance to work on cool things that you should jump at the offer. Keep in mind that your decision will determine how you spend much of your time in the coming months or years. You shouldn't have to make up your mind quickly.

Your response? "I'm glad and honored to hear that you would like to offer me a position. I am excited about working here and I think I can bring great value to the team. This is a big decision for me, however, and I need to think about it."

If offer is low, you might also add: "Frankly, the offer is less than what I understand to be comparable rates in the market, and I need to consider it more carefully. When would be a good time to talk next week?"

Finally, life will not end if you decide to say "no." Indeed, the very same employer might get back in touch. We end with this story to illustrate the point.

Real-Life Story: Emily Brown

For my first job out of college I had a preferred employer, but I was interviewing elsewhere and looking at multiple employers. My preferred employer offered a position that was under my degree qualifications (a secretarial role). I declined the offer for two reasons:

1) It was under my qualifications

2) I was not confident I would be able to get off the secretarial track once on it, even though the employer told me it was a good way to get my foot in the door for other jobs in the company. I did also have some time on my side, so I waited and continued to interview elsewhere.

About two months later, I received an offer from them for an appropriate position. I accepted an offer that was consistent with the market.

Practice Steps

What is your BATNA?

What do you think is their BATNA?

What are your interests?

What do you think are theirs?

What are the hardest questions you think they'll throw your way?

What are your answers?

About the Authors

Paul F. Levy has had an extensive career as a chief executive and leader of several organizations, from running a world-class teaching hospital to managing the multi-billion dollar clean up of the Boston harbor, hailed as one of the most successful examples of public infrastructure projects in a metropolitan area. He has been an innovative leader, known internationally for pushing the boundaries of transparency in organizational communication and continuous learning. He presently advises corporations around the world on negotiation strategy. Paul has enjoyed advising and mentoring college students and young professionals, both during and after his term on the faculty of MIT. He is the author of **Goal Play! Leadership Lessons from the Soccer Field.**

Farzana S. Mohamed is founder and principal of a consulting practice that advises organizations on change management, employee engagement, and process improvement. She previously served as Chief of Staff and Director of Strategic Planning for a community hospital, where she was responsible for managing governance activities and coordinating the planning, user design and permitting for a significant facility expansion, a project that involved interfacing with multiple stakeholders with diverse interests. Farzana was a member of a core management team at MIT involved in setting up two international institutional partnerships. She has worked, lived, and traveled in a number of different countries, and finds negotiation and cross cultural communication fascinating. She enjoys working with and mentoring college students and people just starting out in their careers.

Join us Online!

Please join us at our online community
at negotiateyourjob.com, to share stories about
your own job negotiations and get advice.
Or ask us questions by e-mail at
advice@negotiateyourjob.com.

CPSIA information can be obtained
at www.ICGtesting.com
Printed in the USA
FSOW04n0802010615
7466FS